# DOGS SET XI

# CESKY TERRIERS

Kristin Petrie
ABDO Publishing Company

## visit us at
## www.abdopublishing.com

Published by ABDO Publishing Company, PO Box 398166, Minneapolis, MN 55439.
Copyright © 2014 by Abdo Consulting Group, Inc. International copyrights reserved
in all countries. No part of this book may be reproduced in any form without written
permission from the publisher. The Checkerboard Library™ is a trademark and logo of
ABDO Publishing Company.

Printed in the United States of America, North Mankato, Minnesota.
102013
012014

♻ PRINTED ON RECYCLED PAPER

Cover Photo: Glow Images
Interior Photos: Alamy pp. 5, 7, 9, 11, 13, 21; iStockphoto pp. 14–15, 17, 18–19

Editors: Rochelle Baltzer, Megan M. Gunderson
Art Direction: Neil Klinepier

### Library of Congress Cataloging-in-Publication Data

Petrie, Kristin, 1970-
 Cesky terriers / Kristin Petrie.
    pages cm --  (Dogs)
 Includes index.
 Audience: Ages 8-12.
 ISBN 978-1-62403-101-4
1.  Cesky terrier--Juvenile literature.  I. Title.
 SF429.C37P48 2014
 636.755--dc23
                            2013025485

# CONTENTS

# THE DOG FAMILY

What kind of dog has long, bushy eyebrows and hunts wild boar? It's the Cesky terrier! Cesky terriers are one of more than 400 dog **breeds** found around the world. The **American Kennel Club (AKC)** recognizes more than 150 of these breeds. And, the numbers keep growing!

All dogs are from the family **Canidae**. And, all are descendants of another Canidae member, the gray wolf. Early humans noticed the wolf's superior hunting skills. They tamed and trained wolves to help them track game. This led to the **domesticated** dogs people know and love today.

Over time, humans bred different dogs to get certain features and qualities. Some wanted dogs for herding. Others wanted guard dogs. Still others wanted dogs for hunting in different **environments** and for specific prey.  The Cesky terrier is the result of one hunter's dream for the perfect helper.

Cesky *is pronounced "chehs-kee."*

# CESKY TERRIERS

The Cesky terrier originated in what is now the Czech Republic. There, **geneticist** Frantisek Horak wanted a hardworking dog for hunting small game. This dog needed determination. And, it needed the desire to dive into small tunnels and dens!

In 1949, Horak **bred** a Scottish terrier with a Sealyham terrier. The result was a terrier that would hunt in packs through woodlands and open fields. It had a smaller head and chest than other terriers. So, it was less likely to get stuck when diving into the homes of small game.

The elegant Cesky first spread throughout Europe. Then in the late 1980s, it finally reached the United States. The **AKC** accepted the new breed into the terrier group in June 2011.

6

Ceskies are one of the Czech Republic's national breeds. The dog has appeared on postage stamps, on television, and in books!

# QUALITIES

The Cesky terrier is a natural hunter. It was **bred** to seek small game such as foxes, rabbits, ducks, pheasants, and wild boar. When not hunting, the Cesky loves to dig! Owners must keep their Ceskies entertained to avoid big holes in their yards.

Cesky terriers are highly active and need regular exercise. Yet with enough playtime, Ceskies adapt well to most any **environment**. They can be happy in large homes, in small apartments, on farms, or in cities.

Ceskies are also loving family dogs. In fact, the social Cesky craves attention. They always want to be included in family activities.

*The Cesky is calm, making it a good fit for homes with children and with other pets.*

Despite the Cesky's calm nature, this loyal **breed** is protective of its family. It announces the arrival of strangers with a dutiful bark. Beyond that, the Cesky is reserved with strangers until owners show they can be trusted. **Socialization** throughout its life will keep the Cesky accepting of new people.

# Coat and Color

The Cesky terrier's coat is soft and slightly wavy. Individual hairs are fine but firm. Cesky terriers come in two color varieties. Light brown Ceskies are born chocolate brown. Gray-blue Ceskies are far more common. They are born black. As adults, they come in a range of shades of gray.

The Cesky's **unique** hairstyle is one of its most recognizable features. The standard cut consists of very short hair on the ears, cheeks, tail, and upper torso. Long hair forms the **breed**'s distinctive **fall** and beard. More long, wavy hair flowing from the legs and belly completes the look.

The Cesky's cut serves an important role. Long eyebrows protect the **breed**'s eyes as it dives into fox dens and rabbit holes. Long hair on the legs and belly protects the Cesky as it races through brush and fields.

*Markings on the Cesky's muzzle, chest, legs, and underside can range from white to yellow to rust.*

# SIZE

Cesky terriers are small, compact dogs. They are longer than they are tall. In general, Ceskies stand 10 to 13 inches (25 to 33 cm) at the shoulders. They weigh 14 to 24 pounds (6 to 11 kg). Females are slightly lighter than males.

The Cesky has an **oblong** body with a rounded chest and strong shoulders. The back rises slightly over the rump. The powerful, heavily muscled rear legs are slightly longer than the front legs.

The Cesky has a strong, medium-long neck. This supports a long, blunt, wedge-shaped head. The Cesky's nose is black. The dog's deeply set eyes are brown. Look for them under its long eyebrows!

Medium-sized ears are set high on the Cesky's head. They are long and folded. This protects the inner ear during hunting activities.

The Cesky's tail is generally seven to eight inches (18 to 20 cm) long.

# CARE

Like all dogs, Ceskies need a veterinarian's care. Trained veterinarians provide **vaccines**, checkups, and emergency care. They also **spay** and **neuter** dogs that will not be **bred**.

Dogs also need grooming. The Cesky's hairstyle requires monthly clipping. It leaves long hair on the underbelly, legs, eyebrows, and beard. Frequent brushing of these areas removes and prevents **mats**. Occasional baths with dog shampoo help keep the coat clean, too.

Other grooming includes teeth brushing and nail clipping. Brushing with special dog toothpaste prevents plaque and bacteria buildup. Left untreated, these things can lead to serious infection throughout the body. Nail clipping prevents accidental scratching of furniture, floors, and people!

*Get your dog used to grooming as a puppy. This should make grooming your adult dog much easier!*

# FEEDING

Cesky terriers need a healthy diet and enough calories to fuel their active lifestyles. Many commercial dog foods provide everything they need.

Dog food is available in different varieties. Many owners prefer dry food. It stays fresh longest and helps clean teeth. Others use moist or semimoist dog foods. These provide extra water.

Speaking of water, water is also vital! A small amount comes from moist foods. Yet fresh, clean water must be available at all times for the highly active Cesky.

Ceskies do all or most of their growing during the first year. Young puppies have small stomachs. They need smaller, more frequent meals than grown

16

dogs. Try three or more meals per day.

Experts recommend two larger meals per day for grown dogs. Yet beware! The Cesky loves to eat. Owners must provide the right amount of food in order to prevent unhealthy weight gain.

*Stick with a routine. Feed your Cesky at the same times of day and in the same place each day.*

# THINGS THEY NEED

All dogs need some equipment to live happily in their **environment**. The Cesky appreciates outdoor spaces for running, walking, and playing. This may be a yard, a dog park, or a walking trail. Identification tags and a sturdy collar and leash help keep your dog safe outdoors.

After a long walk, hunt, or playtime, your Cesky will appreciate a place to rest. Dog beds make perfect places to snooze. Dog crates also provide a quiet escape.  These are ideal for travel, as well.  Provide bedding to make them extra cozy.

What else does your Cesky terrier need?  Toys and attention!  This **breed** loves its family.  Puppy toys are perfect for interacting with your new Cesky and meeting its **socialization** needs.  In addition, toys are better to play with than your socks and shoes!

*Ceskies love to play ball!*

19

# PUPPIES

Female dogs are **pregnant** for about 63 days. Like all dogs, Cesky puppies are helpless at birth. They are blind, deaf, and dependent on their mom for 10 to 14 days. Soon after, they begin exploring their surroundings.

Many **breeders** let interested families meet their puppies at 5 to 6 weeks of age. However, puppies must stay with their mother until they are 8 to 10 weeks old. This allows for proper **socialization**, nutrition, and **vaccinations**.

The first meeting is a good time to examine the available puppies. Healthy Ceskies are curious and energetic. They will run to meet you! Be wary of the Cesky that does not join the action or is much larger or smaller than the others. This may indicate a health condition.

20

Once you take your Cesky home, proper training is key. This will lead to good behavior and support **socialization**. Healthy and happy Cesky terriers live more than 10 years.

*At first, puppies drink only their mother's milk. By the time you take your puppy home, it will be eating only solid foods.*

# GLOSSARY

**American Kennel Club (AKC)** - an organization that
studies and promotes interest in purebred dogs.

**breed** - a group of animals sharing the same ancestors
and appearance. A breeder is a person who raises
animals. Raising animals is often called breeding them.

**Canidae** (KAN-uh-dee) - the scientific Latin name for the
dog family. Members of this family are called canids.
They include wolves, jackals, foxes, coyotes, and
domestic dogs.

**domesticated** - adapted to life with humans.

**environment** - all the surroundings that affect the growth
and well-being of a living thing.

**fall** - long hair that hangs over the face of dogs of certain
breeds.

**geneticist** - a scientist who studies genetics. Genetics is
a branch of biology that deals with inherited features.

**mat** - a tangled mass.

**neuter** (NOO-tuhr) - to remove a male animal's
reproductive glands.

**oblong** - longer than broad.

**pregnant** - having one or more babies growing within the body.

**socialization** - adapting an animal to behaving properly around people or other animals in various settings.

**spay** - to remove a female animal's reproductive organs.

**unique** - being the only one of its kind.

**vaccine** (vak-SEEN) - a shot given to prevent illness or disease.

# WEB SITES

To learn more about Cesky terriers, visit ABDO Publishing Company online. Web sites about Cesky terriers are featured on our Book Links page. These links are routinely monitored and updated to provide the most current information available.

**www.abdopublishing.com**

# INDEX